SILVER

FROM 1849 TO 1892

BY

GEO. M. COFFIN,

GREENWOOD PRESS, PUBLISHERS
NEW YORK

PREFACE.

The aim of the writer of this little work has been to present, in a small compass and plain language, an outline sketch of the history of silver since the year 1849, for the convenience of those who have not the time, or the inclination, to gather this information for themselves from its various sources. His effort has been to make it a true and impartial statement of a most interesting subject, the facts and figures for which have been obtained from official documents and other reliable authorities. It also contains some speculations as to the probable effects of a free coinage law from two different points of view.

SEPTEMBER 15. G. M. C.

Originally published in 1892
by McGill & Wallace, Publishers

First Greenwood Reprinting 1969

Library of Congress Catalogue Card Number 69-19665

PRINTED IN UNITED STATES OF AMERICA

SILVER.

1850 to 1860.

As the discovery and production of enormous quantities of gold in California and Australia, beginning with the year 1849, had a most important bearing and influence upon the present position of silver as a money metal throughout the commercial world, no presentation of the silver question as it now exists would be intelligible or fair without proper reference to the main facts as to these gold discoveries.

Some idea of their great importance may be formed from the following comparison of the world's production of gold and silver, respectively, during the ten (10) years ending in 1850 with their production during the next ten (10) years ending with the year 1860:

World's production.	*1841–1850.*	*1851–1860.*
Gold....................	$380,000,000	$1,300,000,000
Silver	350,000,000	400,000,000

From these figures it will be seen that during the last-named period about $900,000,000 more gold was found than during the first, while the product of silver during the latter period had increased by only $50,000,000.

Of course, as the most convenient and exchangeable form for this mass of gold was coin, the owners sent it to the various mints of the world to be coined into money; and so we find that during the ten years ending with 1860 $330,000,000 of gold was coined at the United States mints and about $850,000,000 was coined at the French mints, which, roughly speaking, would account for say $1,150,000,000 of the total world's product of $1,300,000,000 for the same period.

In these days when small silver coins for change circulate so freely in America and the world over, it is difficult to believe that between 1850 and 1860 in this country, and up to 1873 in Europe, these small coins were nearly driven out of circulation through the abundance of gold. The reason for it was that gold had suddenly become so plentiful that by comparison silver became scarcer and dearer, and while the law in the United States made the value of a gold dollar equal to that of a silver dollar, the silver in a dollar piece came to be worth in the markets of the world 101 cents in gold in 1849, and by 1859 the market value had gone up to 105 cents in gold. The money dealers, who always keenly watch the supply and demand of every commodity, soon perceived the great disparity between the supply of the two leading money metals, and the result was that they began to pay a premium over standard value for silver coins, bought and sold them like any other commodity, and this had the effect of driving silver coins out of circulation, thereby causing serious inconvenience by making small change scarce.

In 1834 the United States had by law declared that the value of sixteen (16) ounces of silver was equal to that of one (1) ounce of gold, and had adopted this standard for the coinage of the two metals at its mints; but when it was found that, through the relative abundance of gold, silver coins were being driven out of circulation, it became necessary to take measures to prevent this; so in 1853 a law was passed which provided for the coinage of silver coins smaller than a dollar which would contain less pure silver than the same small coins had before contained. In other words, where two half-dollars, or four quarters, or ten dimes, had formerly contained 371¼ grains of pure silver (the amount in a dollar piece), only $345\frac{6}{10}$ grains of pure silver were now put in these coins. As the effect of this was to make the silver in one dollar of these small coins worth less than one dollar in gold, the money dealers no longer found any profit in them, and they remained in circulation to do duty as small change. The law with regard to the coinage of silver-dollar pieces was left unchanged in 1853, but as France since the year 1803 had coined silver free at the rate of 15½ ounces to 1 ounce of gold, very few silver dollars were coined at the United States mints, where the owner of silver bullion had to give a half ounce more of silver for an ounce of gold, or 16 ounces for one. The increase in the value of silver, as compared with gold, of course had its effect in France also, and we find, therefore, that during the ten (10) years ending with 1860 $278,000,000 of silver was exported or taken out of France, while $636,000,000 of the cheaper gold was imported or brought into that country. Under these circumstances we find that naturally very little silver was coined at the French mints, while, as already stated, about $850,000,000 of gold was coined there. This difference between the net imports ($636,000,000) and the coinage is to be accounted for by the fact that some of the gold was brought in, coined, and afterwards exported again, while large amounts of gold were also used in the manufacture of jewelry.

It is evident that the large amount of silver exported from France ($278,000,000) found its way to India, China, and other eastern countries which then used and still use silver, and not gold, as their chief money metal, for during the ten years ending with 1860 about $460,000,000 in silver was shipped from Europe to India and China. These two countries alone, therefore, absorbed $60,000,000 more of silver than the entire world's product for the ten years ending with 1860, which was, say, $400,000,000. In addition to this mass of silver, it required

$120,000,000 of gold—the *net* amount imported into British India alone from 1851–1860—to pay for the products of India bought by Europe and the nations of the world over and above the commodities sold to India by these nations. In passing it should be noted that in addition to its use as money large amounts of silver are used by the natives of India for making ornaments for personal adornment, and when this habit becomes general in a nation having over 250,000,000 inhabitants it is easy to see that a very small average of silver for each inhabitant would annually absorb a very large amount. Silver so used, too, is practically hoarded as it is taken out of circulation, and so long as this practice continues, as is likely for some time to come, the demand for silver for this purpose, as well as for money, will increase in proportion to the enormous and rapid development of India by means of railways, public works, etc., until a point is reached when, through the general establishment of banks and the use of checks and other instruments of credit, silver will cease to be almost the sole dependence as money for this great beehive of humanity. But as it is estimated that the entire stock of silver money in India is not over $1,000,000,000 at present, or less than $4 to each inhabitant, this ancient people, who are slow to learn the habits of the western world in matters of finance, must for years to come continue to be the great and steady consumer of silver.

The abundant supply of gold which by 1853 had compelled the United States to coin lighter subsidiary silver coin by 1860 had the same effect in Europe, for about this time Switzerland followed practically the same course by putting less pure silver in her smaller coins to keep them in circulation. This was not wholly successful, however, as the cheaper Swiss coins began at once to make their way into France, Belgium, and Italy, and to circulate there, driving out of circulation the French coins which contained comparatively a larger amount of pure silver. This was in accordance with the operation of what is known as Gresham's law, which means practically the putting off upon one's neighbor as soon as one can the cheaper or less desirable money which is in circulation and always keeping the better and more valuable for one's self, or, as it has recently been very aptly defined, it is the law of selfishness.

To protect their people from the invasion of these light-weight Swiss coins, France, Italy, and Belgium held a conference which later on, in 1865, resulted in the formation of what is known as the Latin Union, which also included Switzerland and afterwards Greece and Roumania. Under the terms of this Union the countries forming it agreed jointly on a common ratio of coinage for gold and silver, viz., 15½ to 1, and, like the United States in 1853, also adopted a smaller and uniform weight of pure silver for their subsidiary or smaller silver coins, so as to obviate the previous trouble with these. We have so far not yet made any mention of Great Britain in connection with this subject for the reason that in 1816 she had adopted the single gold standard for her money, coining silver only in limited quantity—silver all this time being bought and sold in the London market as a commodity at varying prices, as it still is at the present time.

In looking back over the history of these ten years one thing is strikingly noticeable, namely, the extent to which the large amount of gold produced during 1851-1860 had been absorbed into the money circulation of the United States and the leading commercial nations of Europe, and the large amount of silver which it displaced—$278,-000,000 from France alone.

From these facts of history it is most reasonable to conclude that these western nations preferred gold to silver as their money of exchange for large commercial transactions on account of the convenience arising from its smaller bulk as compared with silver, and that when so large an amount of silver was discarded by them it found a place waiting for it among the nations of the East whose people had long been accustomed to its use, well knew its value, and to whom it was necessary as a money metal, for the reason that the smaller transactions growing out of a condition of relative poverty compelled the use of the more bulky metal, silver, as money in place of the less bulky and more valuable gold.

As has already been stated in this chapter, the aggregate world's production of the two metals during the ten (10) years ending with 1860 was—

Gold	$1,300,000,000
Silver	400,000,000

The average gold price of the pure silver in a dollar piece (371¼ grains), which was 101 cents in 1849, had risen to 104$\frac{58}{100}$ cents in 1860.

1861 to 1873.

The history of the production, coinage, and movement of gold and silver between 1861 and 1873 will be outlined in this chapter. This period has been selected for the reason that the opening and closing years marked very important eras in the history of silver as a money metal, beginning as it does with the civil war in America in progress and ending with the demonetization of silver by the United States and Germany, the action of the latter nation resulting largely from the outcome of another great war, that between France and Germany in 1870-1871.

Another reason for the selection of this period is the fact that the world's production of gold continued to be large during this time, showing but little decrease towards the end, while the world's production of silver, which was small during the early part, began to increase considerably towards the end.

The following table showing the world's production of gold and silver in the years 1861, 1868, and 1873, respectively, according to the average of figures given by noted statisticians, will better illustrate this:

		Silver.	*Gold.*
World's product'n in	1861,	$45,000,000	$110,000,000
" "	1868,	55,000,000	110,000,000
" "	1873,	70,000,000	100,000,000

According to the average of estimates made by these statisticians the *aggregate* production in the world during the thirteen (13) years ending with 1873 was as follows:

Silver..	$790,000,000
Gold	1,460,000,000

or nearly twice as much gold as silver.

Comparing the production of the first and last years we find that in 1873 the gold product was about 9 per cent. less than in 1861, while the product of silver during the last year was about 55 per cent. greater than it was in 1861.

Of the gold product about $390,000,000 was coined at the United States mints between 1861 and 1873, while $386,000,000 was the *net* amount imported into France, and $320,000,000 represented the *net* imports into British India, which would approximately account for nearly $1,100,000,000 of the aggregate production of the period, the balance being absorbed by other gold-using countries and used in the "industrial arts," or for manufacturing purposes and not as money.

Of the world's product of silver for this period

the *net* imports into France for 1861–1873 were	$121,000,000
The *net* imports into British India for 1861–1873 were	499,000,000
Which together amounted to a total of.......................	$620,000,000

It will be noted what an enormous amount was absorbed by India alone, and this brings us to a most interesting phase of this history.

At the breaking out of the civil war in the United States in 1860 Great Britain and other European nations were large consumers of American cotton. The blockade of the ports of the Southern States, however, almost completely cut off their supplies of cotton from this source, and they were forced to turn to India for a supply. It required large amounts of money to pay for this cotton, and so we find that from 1860 to 1866, during the continuance of the war in America, $359,000,000 of silver was exported from Europe to India and China, about $70,000,000 being exported from France alone during this period. While France was exporting this silver she was importing gold to double the amount, the *net* imports of gold into France during the same time being $147,000,000.

There can be no doubt that the creation of demand for this mass of silver in a new field must have exerted a most potent influence upon the price, for while the world's production of silver during the period of 1860 to 1866 was, according to best authorities, only between fifty and sixty millions a year, gold was flowing into the circulation of commercial nations in large volume. So we find that the average annual price of the silver in a dollar piece varied between 103 cents and 104 cents in gold during 1860 to 1866. After the close of the war in America, and the restoration of trade with the Southern States of the Union, the European demand for cotton from India fell off largely. So after the year 1866 we find that the exports of silver from Europe largely decreased, and in 1867 the average annual gold price of the silver in a dollar piece had declined to 102.67 cents, and, as we shall later see, continued to decline.

Although the trade with India in cotton fell off greatly after 1865, her trade relations with Europe continued to be large and important, and, as this trade had and still has an important connection with the movement of silver, some description of the political and commercial relations between

India and Great Britain are both necessary and appropriate.

As is well known, India has for a long period been subject to the rule of Great Britain. Previous to the year 1858 the country had been governed through the East India Company, but after that the government was transferred to the hands of the Secretary of State of India, appointed by the English Crown, who is assisted by what is known as the India Council, consisting of not less than ten members, all residing in London.

This Council has charge of the collection and disbursement of all the revenues of India, which are mainly derived from taxes on land, opium, and salt.

These revenues have been very large, as will appear from the statement that in 1891 they amounted to the huge sum of about $408,000,000, of which about $115,000,000 was derived from a tax on land, about $40,000,000 from a tax on opium, of which large quantities are produced in India, and about $38,000,000 more from a tax on salt.

Of course as almost the entire money of India is silver, this revenue is collected there in silver. About two-thirds of the revenue collected is now disbursed again in India, but the other one-third is expended in Great Britain and has therefore to be transferred from India to that country. The reason for the transfer of so large a sum of money and the method of transferring it requires some explanation here.

The commercial development of India has required vast sums of money which have been expended for the building of railway lines, irrigation works, and other purposes. Of railways, 16,000 miles had been constructed up to the year 1891, 8,000 miles of these having been built since the year 1879. The money for these purposes has been furnished by Great Britain, and the debt of India to this nation by 1889 had grown to the enormous sum of about $450,000,000. As all these loans were made on a gold basis the interest and principal are of course payable in gold or its equivalent. In addition to the money necessary to pay the interest on this English debt, India has also to provide money to pay English officers in the Indian service and pensioners who reside in England. It is to meet all these demands that one-third of the Indian revenue has to be transferred to Great Britain, and this one-third amounted in 1891 to about $110,000,000 in silver, worth then about $78,000,000 in gold, to which standard it had to be converted when transferred. And now we come to the method of transfer by means of "council bills," about which so much has been heard lately. These are bills of exchange or drafts drawn by the authority of the "India Council" in London on the Indian Treasury. These "council bills" are payable in India in silver "rupees," the money of that country, and are sold in London for their value in gold with which to pay the English creditors of India to merchants or others who have to remit money to India to pay for merchandise, etc., bought there for silver or its equivalent. A rupee is equal in nominal value to two English shillings, or to about 48 cents in United States money. When silver sells in London at 90 cents an ounce in gold a rupee is worth about 32 cents in gold.

If Great Britain had no trade with India, or if what she sold to India was equal in value to what she bought from India, all of this mass of silver, say $78,000,000 worth in 1891, would have actually to be brought from India to England to pay English creditors. Instead of this being the case, however, the value of merchandise exported from India to other countries exceeds the value of the merchandise imported into India from other countries by a very large amount. This difference in value, commonly known as the "balance of trade" of India, amounted in 1891 to about $130,000,000 in gold, and was settled by the remittance of $78,000,000 worth of "council bills," already referred to, and the actual shipment of $52,000,000 (gold value) of silver to India.

The "council bills" drawn in the year 1861, amounted to only $400,000, but as the debt of India to Great Britain increased, the remittances to the latter country for interest on this debt increased also. So we find that the amount of "council bills" drawn between 1861 and 1873 gradually increased, reaching the amount of $69,000,000 in 1873, the last year covered by this chapter. The actual *net* imports of silver into India from 1866 to 1873 amounted to $183,000,000.

Another war occurring toward the close of this period of our history exerted a most powerful influence on silver as money. This was the war between France and Germany, beginning in 1870 and ending in 1871, as the result of which France was compelled to pay to Germany, as an indemnity for losses sustained, the enormous amount of $1,000,000,000 in money. It is said that just previous to 1870 France had been seriously considering the adoption of the single gold standard, but the disastrous result of war placed Germany instead in the position to do this, and this nation promptly availed itself of the opportunity. In 1870 Germany had only about $23,000,000 of gold in circulation, while she had about $375,000,000 of silver. In 1871 she set about completely reversing this order of things, and, having an immense sum of money coming to her from France, on November 23, 1871, passed a law providing for the coinage of new gold coins and *suspending the coinage of large silver coins.* This law also provided for the redemption in gold of the large silver coins issued by the various states of the old German Confederation, which had now combined to form the German Empire instead. The suspension of silver coinage by Germany in 1871 of course closed this market to the producers of silver bullion, and in 1872 we find that the average gold price of 371¼ grains of silver had dropped to 102.25 cents from 102.57 cents in 1871, the world's production steadily increasing all the while. The final action of Germany in 1873, however, appears to have given silver its death blow as a money metal, when in July, 1873, the mint law was passed which established "a national gold standard" in place of that previously existing.

The "mark," worth about twenty-four cents in United States money, was made the monetary unit of Germany, and while the coinage of small silver money was provided for, the amount of pure silver in these new coins was decreased. These silver coins were made legal tender up to the amount of only $5, and the total coinage of same was limited not to exceed in the aggregate more than ten (10) marks (say $2.40) for each inhabitant of the German Empire. It was further provided that before these new silver coins could be issued old silver coins to an equal amount must first have been withdrawn from circulation by redemption in gold. For redeem ing her large silver circulation under the new legislation the indemnity from France provided the gold, about $54,000,000 of the payment being actually made in French gold coin. For the rest she procured the gold from drafts on London given in payment by the French Government. The last of this indemnity was paid over to Germany by France during 1873. In 1873 Germany commenced to sell the bullion produced by melting her old silver coins which she had redeemed with gold, but the effect of these sales on the price of silver will be shown in the next chapter, to which it properly belongs. Before closing this chapter it remains to be stated that the United States also demonetized silver in 1873 by the passage of a coinage law in that year which made no provision for the coinage of the standard silver dollar containing 371¼ grains of pure silver.

The silver interests are now very bitter in their denunciation of those who secured the passage of this law, but only an examination of the records of Congress at the time, showing the debates and progress of the legislation extending over some length of time will enable one to determine whether or not this charge is just. This evidence is too voluminous to be introduced in an outline sketch like this, but in any fair consideration of this phase of the question it is well to bear in mind the following facts: (1) That Germany had more than one year before the passage of this law by Congress suspended the free coinage of large silver coins; (2) that the mints of the Latin Union continued open to the free coinage of silver for about a year after its passage (or until February, 1874), at the higher rate of 15½ to 1; and (3) that in 1873 gold and silver were both at a premium in the United States and not in general circulation; prices being on the basis of a depreciated paper currency and so continuing until January 1, 1879, when specie payments were resumed.

Looking back over this period it is to be noted that during the thirteen years covered by it the world's production of silver had risen from $45,000,000 in 1861 to $70,000,000 in 1873, showing an increase of 55 per cent. in the latter year as compared with the first. The gold price of the silver in a dollar piece, which was $104\frac{58}{100}$ cents in 1860, had declined to $100\frac{46}{100}$ in 1873.

The world's production of gold meantime had declined from about $110,000,000 in 1861 to about $100,000,000 in 1873. The aggregate world's production for the 13 years ending with 1873 was:

Gold	$1,460,000,000
Silver	790,000,000

In Europe a great mass of silver had been ejected from the circulation and its place had been more than filled by a greater mass of gold, and this decline in demand for its use as a money metal with a steadily increasing production would seem fairly to account for the decline in its value as compared with gold.

1874 to 1892.

During the period covered by this chapter the demonetization of silver by Germany which she began in 1871, as already described, was accomplished; the coinage of silver by the Latin Union was first limited and afterwards completely suspended, and an effort was made by the United States, first in 1878 and afterwards in 1890, to restore silver to use as money. As the result of its legislation in 1871 and 1873, Germany commenced in 1873 to sell the bullion into which her old silver coins were converted after their redemption, and from 1873 to 1879, when sales were suspended, it is estimated that she had sold silver bullion to the amount of about $140,000,000 in gold, during which time the gold price of the silver in a dollar piece had declined from the average annual price of $100\frac{46}{100}$ cents in 1873 to $86\frac{96}{100}$ cents in 1879. The natural effect of the suspension of free silver coinage by Germany was to direct the flow of silver to the mints of the Latin Union, which alone of all in Europe or the United States remained open to free coinage, and the result was that during 1873 about $53,000,000 of silver was brought to the mints of France and Belgium for coinage where the year before, 1872, only about $6,400,000 of silver had been coined there. Fearing that this flood of silver, which was declining in value as compared with gold, would take the place of their gold, the Latin Union decided early in 1874 to suspend the free coinage of silver and provided for the coinage of a limited amount. This was followed in 1878 by an agreement by the Latin Union to suspend entirely the coinage of silver. Holland, which was not a member of the Union, entirely suspended silver coinage on July 1, 1875. According to the best authorities it was not only the actual sales of bullion by Germany which tended to depress the price of silver, but in a larger measure the expectation and fear that the amount of bullion so thrown on the market would be much greater than it actually proved to be. Some estimates placed the *net* amount of bullion that would be offered for sale by Germany at say $270,000,000, while as we have stated the proceeds of sales amounted only to about $140,000,000. The effect on the market, however, was just as potent as if that amount had been sold, and the element of uncertainty served to aggravate the situation and affect the price.

All these events had a most depressing effect upon the price of silver, the world's production of which was still steadily increasing, having risen from about $70,000,000 in 1873 to about $95,000,000 in 1878, the production in the United States alone being about $36,000,000 in 1873, and rising to about $45,000,000 in 1878. In this condition of affairs the expulsion of so large an amount of silver from its stock of money by Germany, and the sale of the bullion into which it was melted, had to all intents and purposes the same effect as if this bullion had been taken from the mines and added to the world's production, which outside of this was steadily increasing. In other words, silver had, so far as Europe and the United States were concerned, been shorn of its use as a money metal (except for subsidiary coinage) and was reduced to the condition of a commodity subject, like cotton, wheat, or any other product, to the inexorable and infallible law of commercial supply and demand. During this period, 1873 to 1879, the United States had been passing through a period of severe financial distress and depression growing out of the panic and financial crash of 1873 and the slow and painful process of resuming specie payments after a long period of large issues of depreciated paper currency and the inevitable speculation and extravagance attending same. In 1875 Congress had passed an act providing for the resumption of specie payments on January 1st, 1879, and about 1876 began the popular agitation of the question of remonetizing silver again. This culminated in the passage of the Bland-Allison act of February, 1878, whereby the limited coinage of standard silver dollars containing 371¼ grains pure silver was provided for, and these dollars were made legal tender to an unlimited amount. The act provided that the United States

Treasury should purchase *at its market price* silver bullion to the amount of not less than $2,000,000 worth a month nor more than $4,000,000 worth a month, and for the coinage of this bullion into silver dollars. Under the operation of this law the minimum monthly amount fixed ($2,000,000) was purchased and coined, and from 1878 to 1890, while this act was in force, about 378,000,000 of these silver dollars were coined. As the law provided that the holders of these dollars might deposit them with the United States Treasury in amounts of not less than $10 and receive paper certificates for same, the great bulk of this coin has been held on deposit or storage by the Government, the certificates circulating instead. Without this provision the compulsion to take this bulky coin in the daily transactions of life would have been so burdensome as probably to bring about a repeal of the law. The paper money furnished by means of this coinage happened, too, very opportunely to take the place of National bank circulating notes, which during the same period were withdrawn from circulation by reason of the redemption of the United States bonds, by which the National bank notes were secured, and so the silver certificates served the useful purpose of offsetting the contraction so produced by taking the place of the redeemed National bank notes, which were mostly of the smaller denominations. This brings us to the legislation of 1890, which was the result of the continued agitation of the silver question and of a popular demand for reopening the mints of the United States to the free coinage of silver. The production of silver in the United States had risen from a coinage value of $45,000,000 in 1878 to $64,000,000 in 1889, and meantime the average gold price of the silver in a dollar piece had fallen from about 89 cents in 1878 to about 70 cents in 1889. The world's production, in the meantime, had risen from about $95,000,000 in 1878 to $162,-000,000 in 1889, Mexico contributing $47,500,000 to the aggregate amount in 1889. It was found that in spite of the purchase of $24,000,000 worth of silver bullion every year the price steadily declined. So, as a compromise measure between the silver and anti-silver interests in the United States, an act was passed by Congress on July 14, 1890, which repealed the act of 1878 and provided that the Treasury should purchase 4,500,000 ounces of silver every month at its market price, and for every dollar's worth of silver so purchased $1 in paper should be issued. The notes issued under this act are known as Treasury notes, are legal tender for all private and public debts and payable "on demand in coin." Up to Sept. 1, 1892, $109,382,637 of these notes had been issued for the purchase of silver bullion. The coinage of the bullion purchased under this act into standard dollars has been continued, and 31,721,470 standard dollars have been coined, up to Sept. 1, 1892 leaving about $83,000,000 worth of silver in the Treasury at that date in the form of bars. About the time of the passage of this act the market price of silver had advanced to $1.08 an ounce and under its operation the price of $1.21 an ounce was attained, but this was temporary and the price receded until now (August, 1892) it is worth about 83 cents an ounce. It was hoped that under the effect of these large purchases of 54,000,000 ounces a year by the United States Government, an amount about equal to the annual product of the United States, the price would advance until the market value would equal the mint ratio of $1.29 an ounce, but instead the price has materially declined to a lower point than before the purchases began, and the result has been very disappointing to those interested in silver and has led to a continued agitation for a return to free coinage and to aggressive and earnest debates on the subject in both branches of Congress. During the first session of the Fifty-second Congress the Senate passed a bill providing for the free coinage of silver at the ratio of 16 to 1, but in the House, although two determined efforts were made to pass such a bill, both efforts were defeated by those opposed to the measure. During the seventeen (17) years ending March 31, 1891, India absorbed about $619,000,000 of silver, that being the actual *net* imports of silver into the country, and during the same period of time "council bills" were sold to the amount of $1,158,000,000 besides.

During the period from 1874 to 1891, both years included, the world's production was as follows:

Gold	$1,935,000,000
Silver (coining value)	2,028,000,000

The production of silver at coining value has been as follows:

	World.	*United States.*
In 1874....................	$71,500,000	$37,300,000
In 1891....................	185,600,000	75,416,500

The average gold price of the silver in a dollar piece in 1874 was 98 86/100 cents; in August, 1892, with silver worth 83 cents an ounce, only 64 cents. It will be observed that while the production of silver has largely increased, the aggregate production of gold from 1874 to 1891 has not been very much behind it and of late years has been gradually increasing reaching in 1891 the amount of $125,000,000.

THE FUTURE OF SILVER.

Up to this point we have dealt only with facts and figures taken from the past and sketched a brief outline of the salient points in the history of silver and incidentally of gold since the year 1849. This brings us to the present of a question which greatly agitates the political and financial thought of the United States and to a certain degree occupies the public mind in Great Britain and Europe. We can not with any certainty look into the future of this or any other question, but reasoning from the known to the unknown it is interesting to speculate as to what may happen under certain circumstances.

On the one hand it is claimed by the advocates of free silver coinage that the passage of a law by Congress to this effect would result in raising the market price of silver the world over to the level of the United States mint ratio, 16 to 1, or $1.29 an ounce. On the other side, the opponents of such a measure claim that instead of raising the market price of the world's stock of silver the result would be to depreciate the value of all forms of United States paper currency now in circulation, except gold certificates, to the level of the present market price of silver as compared with gold.

On these two lines, therefore, let us indulge in some speculation.

Assuming first, then, that were a law enacted by the United States making the coinage of silver free at the ratio of 371¼ grains of pure silver in a dollar, or $1.29 an ounce, let us see what would be likely to happen if this had the effect of putting up the price of the metal to $1.29 in the markets of the world where it is now bought and sold as a commodity. In the first place, the owners of silver mines would receive for their bullion about 46 cents an ounce more than they now get for it, say 83 cents.

The world's production of silver in 1891 amounted to about 143,550,000 ounces, worth, at United States mint coinage value ($1.29 an ounce), about $185,000,000, and at market value (August, 1892, 83 cents an ounce) about $119,000,000. If the market price were to advance to $1.29 an ounce the owners of this amount of bullion would receive, say, $66,000,000 more for the year's product than they do at present prices. As the United States produces (at $1.29 an ounce) $75,000,000 a year; Mexico, $53,000,000; the Argentine Republic, $15,000,000; Australia, $13,000,000, and Germany, $7,000,000, or a total of, say, $160,000,000 out of $185,000,000, the gain arising from such increase in price would be chiefly realized by bullion owners in these countries in proportion to the yield in each. Mexico would come in for a large portion, but the lion's share would fall to the United States, where the total production for 1891 was, say, $75,000,000 (coinage value), or 58,330,000 ounces, of which Colorado produced $27,000,000; Montana, $21,000,000; Utah, $11,000,000; Idaho, $5,000,000, and Nevada, $4,400,000. This would mean an annual gain of, say, $27,000,000 on the silver produced in the United States over the amount now received for it, all of which, of course, would go into the pockets of the mine owners of the silver-producing States. This good fortune would surely not be begrudged our fellow countrymen provided it were not obtained at the cost of loss or injury to the country at large. It is needless to say that those persons who produced no silver bullion would not share in this profit. The next phase to consider is what would be the effect on the volume of money in the United States. At present, under the operation of the act of July 14, 1890, 54,000,000 ounces of silver are purchased each year, and this at the present market value of, say, 83 cents an ounce, adds about $45,000,000 (represented by Treasury notes issued for its purchase) annually to the volume of money in circulation. The same amount of bullion, coined at the rate of $1.29 an ounce, would produce, say, $70,000,000 in silver coin, or about $25,000,000 a year more than at present. This amount would be increased, however, if the entire silver product of the United States (58,330,000 ounces in 1891) were coined, and if any considerable portion of the product of Mexico came to our mints to be coined also. In 1891 Mexico produced about $53,000,000 (coinage value) of silver, of which about $38,000,000 was exported, about $14,000,000 of this being imported into the United States in the form of bullion and silver ore, a large portion of the balance being sent to China and other Eastern countries in the form of coined Mexican dollars. As the production of silver in the United States and Mexico has been steadily increasing of late years, although the price has been declining it is most reasonable to assume that any increase in the market value of silver would still further stimulate this production. All of this would, of course, add to the volume of coined silver money in the United States, but the increase would belong to the owners of silver bullion, and nobody would obtain one dollar of it from them except in exchange for a dollar's worth of property, labor, material, or other value received.

Pursuing our inquiry into the effects which would be produced in foreign countries if silver came to be worth $1.29 an ounce, we will not consider such countries as Germany, France, or other European countries where the coinage of silver is not free and where it either serves the purpose of subsidiary coin or is used with gold as the basis of paper currency (as it is in the United States), but will confine our speculations to its effect upon the trade between

Great Britain and India, which latter country is the greatest user and consumer of silver at the present day. It is estimated that the stock of silver money in India at present is about $1,000,000,000, or one-fourth of the entire stock of the world. This stock is being added to every year by large imports of silver into India, the net imports for the year 1891 amounting to about $52,000,000 worth. This silver goes to India from Great Britain and other commercial nations to pay India for the commodities she exports to these countries in excess of the commodities she imports in return from them. A large proportion of her exports consist of wheat and raw cotton, the bulk of which go to Great Britain and consequently Great Britain buys large quantities of silver to pay for these Indian commodities. She buys these Indian commodities at their gold value, although she pays for them in silver, the only money of India, and, of course, if she had to give more gold for the same weight of silver the commodities would cost her more and the result would be as follows: She would be compelled to stop buying wheat and cotton from India and purchase instead larger quantities from the United States, Russia, and other sources of supply. This, of course, would have the effect of stopping shipments of silver to India, which would reduce the volume of money there and at the same time cut off very considerably the demand for Indian cotton and wheat, and the natural and inevitable result would be a fall in the silver prices of these commodities in India until they reached a point where a dollar in gold invested in silver would buy as much as a gold dollar's worth of silver buys now. So far as India is concerned, if the prices of her cotton and wheat and other exportable commodities fell the price of labor and all other commodities for which these are exchanged would fall likewise, so that a smaller volume of money would serve for making exchanges within that country and India would thus arrive at a gold basis. Her commodities on this basis would then compete as now with like commodities from other countries and the general level of these prices would be about what it is now, fluctuating only with increased or decreased supply and demand. Until prices in India declined to the necessary point a temporary increase in the prices of the same commodities in other countries might probably occur, but this would be but temporary, for the pressure to sell Indian produce for export would soon bring about the necessary decline in prices in these days of electricity and steam. In 1890 Great Britain obtained from India only about one-sixth of her entire supply of wheat, so that she is not so largely dependent upon India in this respect as may be supposed. So far as the interests of exporters of English goods to India are concerned, though they would get lower prices in India in silver for their goods, this silver would buy more Indian products in exchange or would buy more gold so that the net result to them would be the same as now. The India Council would be benefited, for their revenue, which is received in silver in India, would be worth more in gold and so would go further toward paying debts in England which are payable in gold.

So much for what would be likely to happen if free coinage in the United States were to increase the market price of silver from 83 cents to $1.29 an ounce. There remains now only the speculation as to what would happen if free coinage in the United States did *not* have this effect, but left the market price of silver in the markets of the world as it is to-day subject to the law of supply and demand, which determines the prices of all other commodities. In the first place, as soon as a free-coinage law was enacted all the silver mined in the United States would naturally go to its mints to be coined, and our next-door neighbor, Mexico, which we have seen now exports about $38,000,000 of silver a year, would be sure to send a large portion of this to our mints if, by so doing, she saw the slightest advantage over present arrangements. Again, it is not known what amount of silver bullion Germany has on hand, or what amount of her old silver coins still in circulation she might redeem and convert into bullion if she saw a good opportunity to exchange this for gold, as she did from 1873 to 1879. It is estimated that there are still about $100,000,000 in German silver coins (thalers) of the old issue in circulation, all the rest, about $275,000,000, having been redeemed. Further, France has about $700,000,000 in silver money, of which about $250,000,000 together with about $300,000,000 in gold is held by the Bank of France as a reserve against its issues of paper money, which circulate at par with gold. As the Bank of France does not hold this stock of silver from choice, but from necessity since Germany demonetized silver and its value as bullion declined, it is not improbable that if the bank saw its way clear to exchanging only a portion, say fifty or a hundred millions of this silver for gold by sending it to the United States mints, it would do so even at a loss of the difference between the two mint ratios, or $1.33 an ounce for the French ratio against $1.29 at the United States mints. The operation would cause a loss to the bank of, say, $4,000,000 on each $100,000,000 so exchanged, but the bank might be willing to meet this loss to procure the gold in exchange if it believed that the price of silver would still go lower. While neither Germany nor France might pursue the course here indicated, the fear of it alone would suffice to produce the same effect as the actual occurrence, as was the case when it was feared that Germany would throw upon the market a much larger amount of silver than she actually did at the time she demonetized silver. In the United States the fear that large quantities of silver might be sent to our mints from abroad to be exchanged for gold to be taken out of the country, though only a fear, would operate first upon the holders of $346,000,000 of legal tender notes which are redeemable in gold, and the holders of some $109,000,000 of Treasury notes issued under the act of July 14, 1890, which are payable on demand "in coin." For the redemption of the $346,000,000 of old "greenbacks" now outstanding a reserve fund of $100,000,000 in gold has been maintained in the United States Treasury since 1879, when specie payments were resumed. Now, official figures show that on July 12, 1892, the National banks alone held $113,915,016 of these legal tender notes or "greenbacks" besides Treasury certificates of deposit for $23,115,000 more of them, a total of, say, $137,000,000 of these notes. Acting upon the impulse of "self-preservation," that "first law of nature" which instinctively moves the masses of mankind, these banks would at the first signal of real or supposed danger from a free-coinage law begin to present these "greenbacks" at the United States Treasury for redemption in gold, and the movement from this source alone would be more than sufficient to exhaust the entire gold reserve of the Treasury. At the same time banks and bankers outside of the National system and money brokers would be actively at work forwarding for redemption such of these notes as they held and gathering up more for the same purpose. The mere beginning of such a movement would precipitate a general rush from all quarters, for the news would be flashed over the country and the commercial world, and as very few of the banks in the United States are more than a week's journey by rail distant from the points of redemption, (New York and San Francisco), it would be possible for these banks and other holders of "greenbacks" to present at least $200,000,000 for redemption within that time, or a sum double the amount of the entire gold reserve. It is true that the Government might sell bonds and borrow gold in this way, but under such circumstances the owners of gold might not be willing to loan in sufficient quantities and promptly enough to enable the Government to meet a sudden emergency except at high rates of interest. The Treasury would have also to be prepared for the redemption in gold of the notes issued under the silver act of July 14, 1890, which on Sept. 1st, 1892, amounted to, say, $109,000,000. It is true that by their terms these notes are payable on demand "in coin," but the moment the Government was unable to redeem them in gold it would amount to a confession of failure to maintain gold payments, and such a condition in a time of financial excitement would be sufficient to put gold at a premium as compared with our other forms of currency, and all payments would then be made in a currency depreciated to the level of a silver basis. The large mass of silver bullion purchased by the Government and now held by it, $83,000,000 on Sept. 1st, 1892, could gradually be coined into silver dollars with which to pay the notes issued for its purchase, but any attempt to sell the bullion in the market for gold would discredit it as a money metal and would have a depressing effect upon its market price by increasing the current supply to the amount sold. As the "greenbacks" and Treasury notes of 1890 would be reissued by the Government as soon as redeemed they could and would be returned for redemption in gold so long as the Government could maintain this, and would, therefore, constitute a menace beyond the total amount now outstanding.

Again, another source of danger exists in the large investments of English and other foreign capital in the stocks and bonds of the various industries of the United States. The fear of receiving a return of this capital or of dividends on same in a depreciated currency would without doubt bring about sales of these securities to a large amount for such prices as they would bring in gold which would be taken out of the country and to that extent decrease the stock of gold in the United States.

The entire stock of gold in the United States on Sept. 1st, 1892, was estimated at $577,000,000, of which the National banks on July 12, 1892, held about $190,000,000, or say one-third of the whole amount. Such gold as was not taken out of the country would be either hoarded, or if loaned, this would be only on obligations payable principal and interest in gold. So long as gold remained at a premium all payments of money by banks, insurance companies, and in fact all money transactions of all kinds in the United States, would be made in silver or in paper currency depreciated below the par value of gold, except where by special contract payment was to be made in gold. Under these circumstances the owners of silver bullion would fare with the rest of the people inasmuch as they would get only silver coin or paper certificates if they sent their bullion to the mints of the United States, or if they sold it in any of the markets of the world, for gold would then as now receive only its value in gold. The state of affairs in the United States would be similar to that existing during the civil war, when all payments were made in legal tenders or "greenbacks" and National bank notes, with this exception, that while both gold and silver then commanded a premium, only gold would have this advantage.

Outside of the United States trade would still continue to be conducted on the basis of the gold standard, as was the case during the civil war, silver being bought and sold in the markets of the world as a commodity.

Looking carefully over the whole situation it would seem that with the market price of silver lower now than it has been for a great many years, the present is a most inauspicious season for the United States, single handed, to undertake to raise the price of the world's stock of silver simply by the experiment of opening its mints to the free coinage of this metal. So far as the production of silver is concerned we have seen that where only about $40,000,000 was produced by the entire world in 1850, the world's product for the year 1891 amounted to $185,000,000, the *aggregate* of the world's production of silver from 1849 to 1891 amounting to the grand total of $3,218,000,000, of which $2,028,-000,000 was produced during the last eighteen years of this period.

In the matter of market price of silver during the same period, we have found that the average annual price of the silver in a dollar piece, which was 101.30-100 cents in gold in 1849, went up to 105.22-100 cents in 1859, and varied between that point and 103 cents until 1866, then remained at about 102 cents until 1872, when it commenced to decline steadily until in August, 1892, it reached at one time the lowest point of, say, 64 cents, or 82½ cents an ounce.

It is a fact that the decline in price is coincident with the increase in supply, and each reader must determine for himself whether or not the cause for such decline is to be found in this enormous increase of supply, aggravated, as we have seen, by a decreasing demand for silver as a money metal and its partial displacement as such by enormous amounts of gold which during the period of our history have been added to the world's stock of money.

The aggregate world's production of gold from 1849 to 1891 has also been enormous, amounting to the grand total of $4,695,000,000, of which $1,935,000,000 was produced during the eighteen (18) years ending with 1891. The world's production of gold, too, shows no signs of decrease, but instead has gradually increased from $96,000,000 in 1873, to $125,000,000 in 1891. With the enormous stock of gold already accumulated and doing service as money, and an annual addition of $125,000,000 to this stock, the reader must also form his own opinion as to the chances of a scarcity of gold for the future.

It is claimed by the producers of silver that at present prices it sells at less than the cost of mining it, and yet the production steadily increases from year to year.

If, as it appears probable, the price of silver has declined with the increase of supply and the decrease of demand, a decrease in the supply should bring about an increase in the price.

It is a poor rule that does not work both ways, and all other efforts to raise the price of silver having failed, the experiment of decreasing the present output of the mines might be tried.

Such a course would afford an opportunity for testing how far the increased production of silver has affected the decline in its price.

As containing matter of general interest in connection with the silver question a few tables have been added as follows:

1. Table showing the stock of money, both metal and paper, in the United States on September 1, 1892.

2. Table showing the estimated stock of such money in various countries of the world at a recent date. In this table the term "uncovered paper" refers to such paper currency as is not represented dollar for dollar by coined money behind it—National bank notes, for instance, in the United States.

3. Table showing the production of gold and silver, respectively, in the world for each year from 1873 to 1891 both inclusive.

[Extract from U. S. Treasury monthly statement, Sept. 1, 1892.]

Statement showing the amounts of Gold and Silver Coins and Certificates, United States Notes, and National Bank Notes, in circulation September 1, 1892.

	General Stock, Coined or Issued.	In Treasury.	Amount in Circulation September 1, 1892.
Gold Coin	$577,737,991 00	$166,583,580 00	$411,154,411 00
Standard Silver Dollars	414,966,735 00	357,343,849 00	57,622,886 00
Subsidiary Silver	77,472,912 00	13,575,773 00	63,897,139 00
Gold Certificates	152,234,589 00	23,847,210 00	128,387,379 00
Silver Certificates	331,068,304 00	2,779,159 00	328,289,145 00
Treasury Notes, act July 14, 1890	109,382,637 00	5,268,551 00	104,114,086 00
United States Notes	346,681,016 00	29,132,596 00	317,548,420 00
Cur'y Cert'f's, act June 8, 1872	22,770,000 00	560,000 00	22,210,000 00
National Bank notes	172,656,429 00	6,623,311 00	166,033,118 00
Totals	2,204,970,613 00	605,714,029 00	1,599,256,584 00

Table exhibiting, approximately, the stock of money in the aggregate in the principal countries of the world.

Countries.	Population.	Stock of gold.	Stock of silver.	Uncovered paper.
United States	65,000,000	$687,000,000	$556,000,000	$422,390,000
United Kingdom	38,000,000	550,000,000	100,000,000	30,530,000
France	39,000,000	900,000,000	700,000,000	81,402,000
Germany	49,500,000	500,000,000	205,000,000	107,000,000
Belgium	6,100,000	65,000,000	55,000,000	54,000,000
Italy	31,000,000	93,605,000	50,200,000	163,471,000
Switzerland	3,000,000	15,000,000	15,000,000	14,000,000
Greece	2,200,000	2,000,000	4,000,000	14,000,000
Spain	18,000,000	100,000,000	125,000,000	94,000,000
Portugal	5,000,000	40,000,000	10,000,000	6,000,000
Austria-Hungary	40,000,000	31,330,000	90,000,000	260,000,000
Netherlands	4,500,000	25,000,000	65,000,000	40,000,000
Scandinavian Union	8,600,000	32,000,000	10,000,000	27,000,000
Russia	113,000,000	190,000,000	60,000,000	500,000,000
Turkey	33,000,000	50,000,000	45,000,000	....
Australia	4,000,000	100,000,000	7,000,000	....
Egypt	7,000,000	100,000,000	15,000,000	....
Mexico	11,600,000	5,000,000	59,000,000	2,000,000
Central America	3,000,000	....	500,000	2,000,000
South America	35,000,000	45,000,000	25,000,000	300,000,000
Japan	40,000,000	90,000,000	50,000,000	56,000,000
India	255,000,000	....	900,000,000	28,000,000
China	400,000,000	....	700,000,000	....
The Straits	....	....	100,000,000	....
Canada	4,500,000	16,000,000	5,000,000	40,000,000
Cuba, Hayti, etc	2,000,000	20,000,000	2,000,000	40,000,000
Total	....	3,656,935,000	3,944,700,000	2,281,793,000

Statement of Bureau of the Mint, Treasury Department, *May* 24, 1892, made to Congress.

[Report of Director of Mint, U. S., for 1891.]

Production of Gold and Silver in the World for the Calendar Years
1873-1891.

Calendar years.	Gold.	Silver.	
	Value.	Fine ounces (troy).	Coining value.
1873	$96,200,000	63,267,000	$81,800,000
1874	90,750,000	55,300,000	71,500,000
1875	97,500,000	62,262,000	80,500,000
1876	103,700,000	67,753.000	87,600,000
1877	114,000,000	62,648,000	81,000,000
1878	119,000,000	73,476,000	95,[illegible]00,000
1879	109,000,000	74,250,000	96,000,000
1880	106,500,000	74,791,000	96,700,000
1881	103,000,000	78,890,000	102,000,000
1882	102,000,000	86,470,000	111,800,000
1883	95,400,000	89,177,000	115,300,000
1884	101,700,000	81,597,000	105,500,000
1885	108,400,000	91,652,000	118,500,000
1886	106,000,000	93,276,000	120,60[illegible],000
1887	105,775,000	96,124,000	124,281,000
1888	110,197,000	108,827,000	140,706,000
1889	123,489,000	125,420,000	162,159,000
1890	120,475,000	134,380,000	173,743,000
1801	125,300,000	143,550,000	185,600,000